House Beautiful

Slipcovers

House Beautiful

Slipcovers

THE EDITORS OF HOUSE BEAUTIFUL MAGAZINE

■ ■ ■

TEXT BY
SALLY CLARK

HEARST BOOKS

A DIVISION OF

STERLING PUBLISHING CO., INC.

NEW YORK

Copyright © 1994 by Hearst Communications, Inc.

Edited by Laurie Orseck
Interior design by Nancy Steiny
Cover design by Deborah Kerner, Dancing Bears Design

Produced by Smallwood & Stewart Inc., New York City

■   ■   ■

Library of Congress Cataloging-in-Publication Data
Available upon request.

10 9 8 7 6 5 4 3 2 1

First Paperback Edition 2003
Published by Hearst Books
A Division of Sterling Publishing Co., Inc.
387 Park Avenue South, New York, NY 10016

House Beautiful and Hearst Books are trademarks owned by
Hearst Magazines Property, Inc., in USA, and Hearst Communications, Inc., in Canada.

www.housebeautiful.com

Distributed in Canada by Sterling Publishing
c/o Canadian Manda Group, One Atlantic Avenue, Suite 105
Toronto, Ontario, Canada M6K 3E7
Distributed in Australia by Capricorn Link (Australia) Pty. Ltd.
P.O. Box 704, Windsor, NSW 2756 Australia

Printed in China

ISBN 1-58816-229-X

C O N T E N T S

FOREWORD

*t*he offhand chic and unstudied elegance of slipcovers—the classic "saviors" of interior design—can dress up or dress down a room, alter the lines of furniture, recolor or add pattern to tired spaces. Traditionally used to work a seasonal change and protect upholstery, slipcovers can also undercut the set, molded look of conventional pieces.

As Sally Clark writes in the text that follows, taste in slipcovers is changing. One of those changes is unexpected material choices—terry cloth on seating for a bath or dressing room, for example, or see-through fabrics that let the tracery of wicker or wood show through. One of the chicest rooms we've seen had the surprise of black linen covers on an Early American camelback sofa and traditional chairs.

But slipcovers aren't only for seating. A tailored cloth can cover a tired table without sacrificing the storage underneath; even walls can be "slipcovered" by simply hanging a handsome fabric from a track installed around the perimeter of the room. And for the simplest treatment of all, just change the covers on your pillows to see the magical powers slipcovers really have. We guarantee it will be only the beginning.

—THE EDITORS, *HOUSE BEAUTIFUL*

INTRODUCTION

*t*here would be little reason to devote a design book to slipcovers if they were only practical handmaidens of decoration, defending furniture against sunlight and wear. But as stylish implements of change, they are decorating's secret weapon. Their almost magical power has always been valued by designers. They can dress up or dress down a chair or sofa; by their cut and construction they can alter the lines of the furniture they cover, lending grace to an oddly proportioned chair and modernity to a vintage sofa. They can totally, and instantaneously, recolor a design scheme. And they can apply pattern where minutes before none existed.

Slipcovers are accessible to every budget, whether casually run up in store-purchased fabric or meticulously tailored in decorator material in a professional workroom. Some are not even sewn at all, but are just lengths of colorful fabric creatively draped and tucked over a chair or sofa frame and cushions. The renowned firm of Parish-Hadley once caused a stir at a New York City showhouse by doing a room entirely in red and white pinstriped cotton slipcovers. "They were just bags," says Albert Hadley, "the

kind you would put over the furniture in the summer." But compared to the other rooms in the showhouse, which were filled with stiff, tautly upholstered furniture, the loose covers casually dropped over Victorian chairs were a sensation. In its light cheerful look, the room could have been inspired by nineteenth-century watercolors showing slipcovered furniture.

Fashion has always been a rich source of inspiration for slipcovers. The construction of clothing, as well as the fringes, buttons, and trims that are part of the dressmaker's art, provides enormous possibilities for creating every shape and style of slipcover.

We hope *House Beautiful Slipcovers* will become yet another major source of inspiration for you. It is filled with solutions devised by professional decorators throughout the country, from the single little chair to entire rooms dramatically transformed. All are intended as inspiring models. By translating and adapting the shapes and decorative details shown in these pages, you will be able to use slipcovers to bring a highly personal and stylish look to every room in your home.

OFFHAND CHIC

As powerful elements of decoration, slipcovers are capable of altering the style and mood of furniture and entire rooms. Reasons of beauty and function have long encouraged their use in interior decoration. Billy Baldwin, the renowned American decorator, always championed their high-fashion power. He often designed not just one but two sets of slipcovers for clients so that the whole look of a room could be dramatically transformed each season simply by a change of fabric. Now other American designers are taking a leaf from his decorating scrapbook, adding their own ideas and creating marvelously fresh interpretations. One designer drapes a giltwood chair with gauzy linen to achieve an ethereal accent in a living room. Another outfits vintage upholstery in loose-fitting cotton cover-ups to evoke an old-world ambience in a house too young to have its own heritage. Slipcovers bring to any decorating scheme an unstudied elegance and luxuriant ease that is thoroughly compatible with the American sense of style and relaxed way of living. ❁

Timeless and Timely Decorating

Slipcovers undoubtedly came into being the first time someone in the ancient world created a comfortable place to sit by draping a wooden bench with a flat-weave carpet or a piece of tapestry. In medieval and Renaissance Europe, when furniture was scarce and frequently moved from room to room, removable cushions eased the hardness of wooden stools and chairs and introduced color and suppleness to nearly empty interiors. Simple tailored slipcovers appeared in wealthy English households in the eighteenth century to protect chair seats covered in then-rare and costly silk brocades. By the nineteenth century, covers of brightly printed cottons were popular in Europe and America as a stylish decoration as well as a shield against dirt and sunlight.

Protecting expensive seating is just one use of slipcovers. "You can experiment with different decorating possibilities without having to reupholster," says Manhattan designer Vicente Wolf. By suiting upholstery in new ~ and removable ~ colors and patterns, it is possible to obtain a fresh look without the much greater expense and inconvenience of reworking the whole room. With all the different ways slipcovers can be cut, draped, and sewn, they are a versatile disguise for mismatched or worn-out chairs and sofas. With a floaty cotton cover-up a modern Eames chair turns traditional, a metal chair looks upholstered, and a formal damask sofa relaxes. This wizardry can even transform other furnishings, turning an inexpensive table into a comely chintz-draped vanity or tapestry-cloaked console.

Slipcovers have always been used to work a seasonal change. To cope with the heat in the days before air-conditioning, slip-ons of cotton were eased over permanent upholstery, often made of scratchy mohair or thick jacquard; light cotton cover-ups are still a summer tonic on a sultry day. The billows, drapes, and tucks of slipcover fabric can also take the hard edges off a modern room and compensate for the emptiness of a spare one. In addition, mixing covered pieces with upholstered ones, says Wolf, can effectively undercut "the set, molded look of conventional upholstery," bringing in "a casual, off-the-shoulder quality." In decorating, a bit of offhand chic is always welcome.

Slipcovers of white cotton in a twill weave soften the rigid lines of the French provincial armchairs circling a library table. Atlanta decorator Dan Carithers underplayed the formality of the chairs by attaching long dangling ties as fasteners. So deep are the seats that he added a luxurious separate back cushion to each.

For a Connecticut week-end house, designer Beverly Ellsley recycled upholstered dining room chairs by dressing them in tailored slipcovers of textured beige cotton. The neutral color was the ideal choice in a room dominated by the natural wood tones of the pine floor and the full-length doors of a pine cupboard. Pulling up an unmatching metal garden chair to the table injected contrasting shape and texture into the ensemble.

In an elegant New Orleans town house, designers Ann Holden and Ann Dupuy put a casual twist on a formal setting by dropping cotton canvas slipcovers over Louis XVI chairs. The loosely constructed cover-ups are styled after those used in the eighteenth century to protect chairs upholstered in costly silk brocades.

In a setting dominated by leafy wallpaper and natural textures, an old metal chair takes up residence under a dust cover of botanical-patterned cotton. A pillow cover made from cotton in a leafy print and a tiny stool of twigs and moss are captivating accessories plucked from nature.

To introduce a sense of age to a 1960s Los Angeles house, designer Lynn von Kersting brought in vintage upholstery from the 1920s and 1930s and covered it in slipcovers made from old French linens and cottons. The peppermint-striped cotton cover-up on the reading chair is constructed with the stylish sloppiness of the ones traditionally used in English country rooms.

Summer coolers: The wool tapestry upholstery that cozied up designer Mary Emmerling's sofas in January was unbearable to sit on in June, so she had slipcovers made from a muted cotton print of lush bouquets framed in overscale cartouches (above). She also popped cover-ups on the ottomans ~ green and white checked cotton on one, a persimmon and cream-colored cotton print on another.

Designers Charles Spada and Tom Vanderbeck slipcovered a sofa in cool matte gray-green linen, outlined it in gray-green silk cording, and added downy pillows in gray-green silk damask and mushroom-colored taffeta (right). Bare floors and sheer French cotton gauze at the windows also make the room "wonderfully cool," says Spada.

Decorator Beverly Field brought the oldest form of slipcovering to her living room by draping a sofa with an Indian throw, then heaping on pillows made from exquisite antique silks and tapestries (opposite). The easy chair near the fireplace is cloaked in an Indian cotton quilt she bought in Paris (left). Keeping all the fabric throws in predominating tones of red results in a successful mix of textiles from different countries and periods. Blue and white carpets complete the look of a Moroccan haven in an orientalist painting, the genre of art that inspired the designer's decor.

Giving the Seasons Their Due

With its sun-dappled walls, overstuffed chairs enveloped in sensuous damask, antiques garnered in Paris and Rome, and generally insouciant air, the house looks like a villa in the south of France in the 1930s. But this is southern California, the time is now, the view is of the Pacific. "I wanted to make it more evocative, like the old beach houses," says Beverly Hills designer Michael Smith of the stark, contemporary house that he transformed into these romantic surroundings. Slipcovers helped him create a feeling of languid elegance; fabrics like damask and a cotton and linen tea-stained English floral, readily associated with European decor of previous eras, were his medium.

The living room wears two distinct seasonal looks. In a reversal of the traditional use of slipcovers, the sofa and chairs breeze through the summer in their permanent green and white striped cotton upholstery. It isn't until the fall and winter that cover-ups of celadon Fortuny cotton damask are added to the custom-made easy chairs. The sofa is dressed in a lush tea-stained floral in cotton and linen. These fabrics, traditionally used in European drawing rooms of

By selecting fabrics with bright scarlet touches, designer Michael Smith successfully meshed three very different fabric patterns in the study of this contemporary California house. The red and white striped cover-up on the rattan chair is an unexpected bit of boldness among the florals.

the 1920s and 1930s, lend the room a patina of the past. To warm up the space even more in winter, Smith lays an antique kilim area rug over the sisal matting and brings in a tapestry-covered ottoman as a coffee table. A Venetian grotto chair of gilded wood is a wonderfully eccentric accent. As rich details on all the seating, Smith designed downy decorative pillows covered in scarlet and artichoke-colored damask.

The floaty white cotton slipcovers in the bedroom, however, stay in place through all seasons. Their year-round purpose is to bring allure to a room that Smith deemed an unimaginative "modernist shell" when he first saw it. To create a dreamy mood, he glazed the walls of the room yellow, which casts a glow of perpetual sun, and draped the steel canopy bed with diaphanous white-on-white paisley cotton. He upholstered the cushy custom sofa, easy chair, and ottoman in white cotton muslin, then covered the permanent upholstery with billowy covers of lightweight tablecloth damask ~ "soft, blowy, and romantic, like little ball gowns," says Smith. Such fragile fabric is fine for bedroom seating, which doesn't get hard use. Although the light covers seem to float like fine handkerchiefs on the upholstery, they depend on expert cut and construction. Several well-placed welts ~ the fabric-covered cord running around the edges, under the arms, and at the skirt seams ~ help anchor the slipcovers and define the lines of the furniture underneath. "If a sofa or chair is well made and has a beautiful form, I like the slipcover to have some structure that hints at the shape of the upholstery," the designer explains. In the glowing yellow room, the breezy covers, made in the slightly loose European style, create an image of a bygone time ~ which is indeed the romantic spell Smith intended to cast.

Made from medium-weight fabrics that drape well, the slipcovers used in the cooler months have a luxurious yet dressed-down look (above). The mood lightens up in summer, when the slipcovers, along with the kilim rug and most of the throw pillows, are removed (opposite). Roman blinds of green and white striped cotton are a year-round window treatment.

The fine cotton slipcovers in the bedroom barely graze the sisal floor matting. "Slipcovers that are too loose look like an ill-fitting dress," designer Smith says. "I don't like skirts to fall on the floor because the flounces may get ripped." The series of welts he devised hug the shape of the furniture and hold the slipcovers in place at the same time. Conch shells perched on a side table and on wall sconces are whimsical allusions to the Pacific Ocean, visible through the French doors.

MATTERS OF STYLE

Slipcovers come in as many styles and shapes as there are styles and shapes of furniture on which to put them. Often, the design of the chair or sofa will influence the design of the cover-up. A tufted Victorian chair begs to be romanced by a ruffle-skirted slipcover, just as a tuxedo sofa demands a crisp, unfussy shape. Sometimes designers reverse the process: They intentionally do not match slipcover to chair style, either to update an outmoded look or camouflage a piece of a very specific design ~ disguising a Louis XVI chair under a baggy linen slip-on gives it a casualness that may be desirable when it is moved to a less formal setting. However, in an elegant room, the slipcover of choice for the same French chair might be a damask tie-on that exposes the beautifully carved wooden frame, in perhaps an offbeat color such as chartreuse or lavender. With slipcovers, so many styles are possible. It all depends on the chair, the setting, and one's own imagination. ✹

Cut to Fit: From Tailored to Baggy

The two most popular categories of slipcover styles are loose and tailored. Nations seem to draw up sides on the question, with the English favoring baggy slipcovers, while the Americans prefer them crisply tailored. Loose-fitting slipcovers that look like dustcovers have been popular for generations in English country houses, popped over the seating and draped in a fashionably sloppy manner. By contrast, the American slipcover favored by designers such as Billy Baldwin has always been streamlined and, with the help of well-concealed zippers, fits neat as a pin. A distinctive detail of the tailored American-style cover-up is the welt, a fabric-wrapped cord outlining the slipcover seams. Always cut on the bias, which has more give, the welt also serves a structural function in reinforcing the seams, especially important on these snug-fitting cover-ups, which are subject to the pulling and tugging of everyday use. The welt can be made from the same fabric as the slipcover, or it might sound a decorative note in a contrasting color and pattern.

In recent years, influenced by the popularity of the English country-house style, some American designers have relaxed the fit on the slipcovers they make for clients. Yet no matter how nonchalant these cover-ups seem, they usually depend on sophisticated, well-concealed structural elements. In his furniture-skimming creations, John Saladino achieves fit through meticulous cut and tidy seams. Michael Smith's flowing and romantic loose cover-ups are "supported" by a well-devised network of welts.

Between these extremes of loose and tailored are any number of styles and variations ~ tiny as an apron on a dining room chair, voluminous enough to cover an entire sofa; sleek and snug as a leotard thanks to snaps, buttons, zippers, and Velcro, or baggy as a sack with no closures at all.

Inspiration for slipcover styles and details comes from many sources. Fashion is a major influence, which is not surprising considering the close relationship between the upholstery arts and dressmaking. Designer Vicente Wolf actually considers slipcovers "garments" and speaks of different "bodies that you can dress up or down depending on the details you add." John Saladino describes the fabric ties on the slipcovers he designs as "haute couture" elements.

The simple sacklike shape of these unadorned chair covers is a classic style that was especially popular in the eighteenth century. Their contemporary elegance derives from the fabric, a cotton and linen blend printed with a luxurious damask pattern in tones of rose accented by a broad band of aqua.

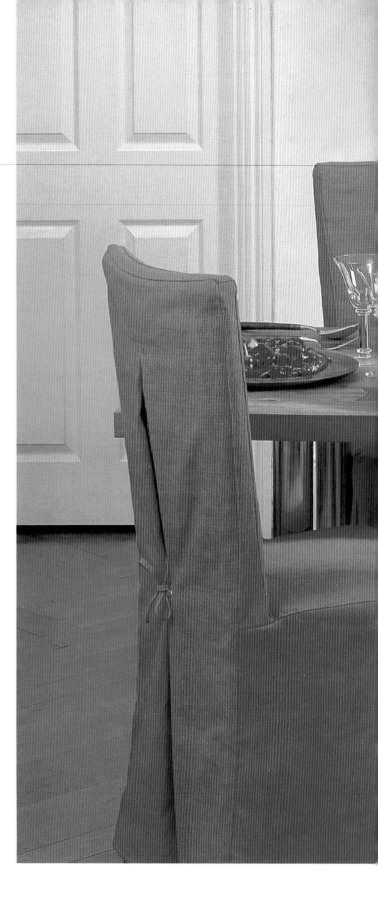

A deep inverted pleat caught with a string bow tie adds rakish flair to the slipcovers on these straight-back dining chairs. The home-owner had the slip-ons made of nubby-weave red cotton for her London apartment.

To make properly tailored slipcovers, which should be hand cut and hand fitted to the individual chair or sofa much like a custom-made suit, the skill of a professional may be required. On the other hand, loose-fitting slipcovers are not difficult for the nonprofessional to run up on the sewing machine, especially for someone with experience making dresses from patterns. The fun is in trying out shapes and trims from the ocean of ideas that dressmaking provides.

The owner of a New England weekend house took a tailored approach to cooling down a room enjoyed mostly in summer (opposite). Using quilted white muslin that cost less than $5 a yard, she hugged the lines of the armless Victorian chair, secured the unadorned cover with Velcro, and finished it with a simple hem.

In a Long Island beach house (above), loose-fitting cotton canvas slipcovers protect the cushy sofa and easy chair from the daily wear and tear of damp bathing suits and sandy feet; a run through the washing machine keeps them looking fresh. Designer Vicente Wolf had the covers cut and sewn in a loose style that matches the easy elegance of the white-on-white bedroom.

For her formal
eighteenth–century–style
armchairs, artist
Marilyn Caldwell created
slipcovers of white cotton
duck that fit like pillow-
cases (opposite). She
used long loopy ties as
a humorous detail.

Manhattan designers
Joseph Lembo and
Laura Bohn outfitted a
regally proportioned
slipper chair with a
snug-fitting back and seat
cover contrasted by a
billowing skirt (above).
The slipcover's filmy

polyester material
might easily be
mistaken for silk.

Designers Ronald
Mayne and De Bare
Saunders tied a white
cotton terry-cloth apron
to the seat of a little giltwood chair, draping it
langorously over the sides
(right). The fabric is
banded in brandy-
colored silk and anchored
at the front corners by
appliquéd lozenges of the
same material.

As a contrast to the crisp-edged modernism of his duplex home in Washington, D.C., designer Gary Lovejoy likes the "almost cloud-like" feeling of yards of draped cotton on his contemporary furniture. In the bedroom (above), he tucked striped cotton sheets between the uphol-stered seat and back of Donghia chairs, then artfully draped the excess yardage. The white cotton sheets on two dining room chairs (opposite) are fastened together with snaps at the bottom so they hold a flared shape not unlike a ghostly costume.

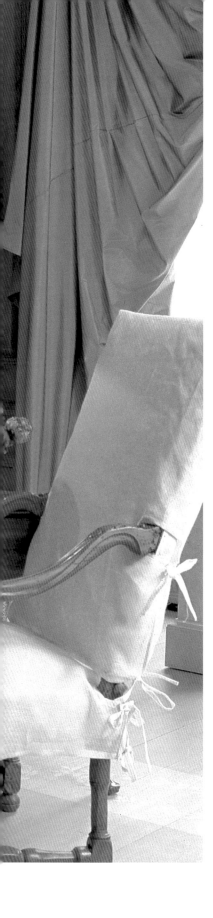

Putting a Formal Room at Ease

In a neo-federal red brick house built in the 1920s, the original drawing room was a salon of grand proportions and high ceilings. Upholstered furniture would have been as predictable in this wood-paneled room as yards of fringed velvet curtains. One glance at the room, however, and New York designer John Saladino realized that a more imaginative, and more provocative, approach was to go completely against the grain of the stately architecture. Instead of predictable velvet and tapestry permanently molded on the furniture, he chose lightweight cotton, silk, and linen for slipcovers and loosely draped curtains. Those decisions, says the designer, introduced a spontaneous quality that "took the thunder out of the palace" and completely relaxed the formal room.

In place of a standard furniture arrangement ~ traditional roll-arm sofa and easy chairs ~ Saladino pulled up furniture from different centuries and points of view. He teamed a seventeenth-century English high-back armchair with a contemporary

In a series of unexpected pairings, designer John Saladino put a baroque English chair next to a modern sofa, then dressed the chair in a thoroughly contemporary slipcover of plain white linen and the sofa in periwinkle cotton. On both pieces, he spaced the fastening ties so that they serve as a decorative detail that teases the eye.

high-back sofa of his own design. He also slid one of his upholstered tub chairs into a grouping with a nineteenth-century Grecian sofa and antique painted chair. Then he threw a real design curve: In the center of the room he placed a borne, a custom-made version of the upholstered island often used in Victorian hotel lobbies.

The slipcovers, which share a pale palette and details like cords and ties, became the room's unifying motif. For the tub chair, Saladino designed a tailored cotton damask cover-up in a color he calls frosted amethyst. The island is clad in gauzy ivory linen; parchment-colored cording ending in fat tassels finishes off the corners of the back pillows and the four corners of the seat; and the skirt is edged in a beige cotton tape from which dangles a row of wooden baubles. The remaining slipcovers ~ slightly transparent ivory linen for the seventeenth-century chair and periwinkle cotton for the sofa ~ are fastened with a series of fabric ties ("not unlike a repeating melody," Saladino explains) whose exact placement was specified in the designer's sketches. Precisely constructed and loosely knotted, the slightly floppy ties carry the subtlest suggestion that they might easily come undone. They are details that seem to say that this salon, despite its palatial scale, is definitely not stuffy.

A cotton slipcover tinted an icy lavender hugs a tub chair that Saladino designed; resting on the seat of the painted chair is a silk cushion in a soft lavendar, banded in satin. In the foreground is a Victorian-style upholstered island. The flowing curtains are made of unlined iridescent silk taffeta that ranges from gray to raspberry tones.

PERSONAL PANACHE

the expression of personal style always seems to involve an element of surprise. In the case of slipcovers, it might be the choice of a novel fabric, perhaps a print with a sense of humor. Or a fabric might be used in an unexpected way, such as thick terry-cloth toweling pulled over a sofa in a master bathroom. The shape might be an unusual one, resembling a dramatic cloak or a dropped-waist chemise, for example, or "the slipcover" might be nothing more than a giant square of fabric tied around a chair like a scarf. The inspiration for devising a slipcover with great panache can come from many sources. One designer takes his cues for dining chair covers from the dress silhouettes of famous couturiers. His "Chanel" has a kicky pleated skirt and a row of buttons down the back, while his "Balenciaga" turns a straight-back chair into a statuesque profile in taffeta. A single elegantly covered chair can lend a decorating scheme instant flair. A room filled with seating dressed in unusual slipcovers is a confident statement of individual style. ❁

Self-Expression

The witty and offbeat slipcover shapes that decorators have worked out professionally certainly offer ideas and models that can be emulated ~ Nancy Braithwaite brings a startling sculptural presence to her interiors, for example, while Jeffrey Goodman and Steven Charlton look to Italian pageantry for inspiration.

However, inventing clever looks and treatments is not solely in the professional's realm. A willingness to experiment, aided by one's own talents and passions, can achieve the most remarkable results. The Sunday painter might decorate canvas with lively brushwork; the amateur seamstress appliqués chintz flowers on a slipcover hem; the collector of old textiles wraps the living room chairs in paisley throws ~ the possibilities are endless. And if one invention eventually grows tiresome, it can always be changed, which is after all the chief blessing of slipcovers.

The unsewn slipcover: Artfully draped fabric creates stylish chair covers in a Milan living room (opposite and right). Angela Maccapani used unmatching lengths of fabric, one a radiant print dominated by pinks, the other mostly blue, to wrap up two club chairs; a third print, in orange and black, was draped on a sofa. The build-up of colors and patterns shows the same genius for design as the unique knits for which Missoni, Maccapani's family business, is famous.

Three different patterns of faded 1940s floral chintz bloom on the sofa in Ellen O'Neill's New York City apartment. A stylist and collector of vintage textiles, O'Neill mixed the prints with a sure hand, counting on the shared tones of red and the large scale of all the flowers to tie the different fabrics together. To achieve a layered look, she draped a white-on-white vintage bedspread over the sofa back, then arranged square and heart-shaped chintz pillows against it.

Completely unadorned, a cotton ticking slipcover is constructed to fit snugly over a Regency "bath-tub" sofa. The severity of the unskirted treatment is softened by a heap of inviting cushions covered in snappy checked and striped cottons.

By folding a Mexican saltillo ~ a finely woven antique textile of wool and silk ~ over a seat pad, textile designer Chris O'Connell created an instant slipcover and turned an Old West daybed into an unusual sofa for her Santa Fe condominium. Throw pillows piled along the back and at each end add a note of soft comfort. The pillows are also covered in Mexican saltillos, making the daybed a showpiece of zesty southwestern color and style.

Slipcovers made of cotton in two brilliant colors were inspired by the flags of Siena's famous Palio horse race (left). Designers Jeffrey Goodman and Steven Charlton dreamed up the offbeat furniture costumes to adapt flea-market chairs to their riotously colored dining room.

Decorator Mary Douglas Drysdale needed a tall thin element to finish off a room scheme (opposite). A tapering chair by Scottish architect and designer Charles Rennie Mackintosh was the perfect height but the wrong look until Drysdale transformed it with a cotton chintz popover appliquéd with black diamonds.

A Touch of New England Down South

Atlanta designer Nancy Braithwaite believes that "if a room has power it can stand on its own," unaided by bibelots and bric-a-brac. She pushed that personal conviction to the edge in decorating her own house. In barely accessorized rooms, overscale upholstery, all of it cloaked in slipcovers, is an intentionally august presence, providing much of the "power" Braithwaite finds so satisfying in an interior.

The house, designed in 1964 by the celebrated Atlanta architect James Means, is a classic saltbox with low-ceilinged rooms accentuated by antique beams and floorboards. In the landscape of New England it would be right at home. But in the nearly tropical Deep South, the house, built with dark interiors, looks unusual, almost foreign. For most people the temptation would have been to open up and lighten the rooms. Braithwaite, who bought the house in 1992, actually started to do that, but soon realized she was contradicting Means's architecture and intention. Instead, she decided to let the sober New England spirit that Means captured so well in the shadowy rooms be her design muse as well.

To slipcover her dining room chairs with "a very textural look," designer Nancy Braithwaite chose a loosely woven linen. The fabric, an impractical choice for chairs subjected to hard wear, works well here for the special-occasion dinner party. To emphasize the unusual shape of the chairs, the designer ran a thick tubular welt around the edges.

Economy of detail is everything in this house. In the spare rooms that she envisioned, Braithwaite knew she would need large forms to fill space and energize it. To achieve the look she wanted, she had overscale sofas and chairs custommade. All the upholstery was finished off in plain muslin, then dressed with simply cut slipcovers in neutral-colored fabrics ~ beige, cream, white, and black ~ with very pronounced textures.

Before installing the furniture, Braithwaite set the stage. To pick up the flavor of the architect's antique finishes, she gave the walls a subtle textural treatment with a thin coat of plaster, then applied somber colors suggested by old New England walls. The dining room was painted with layers of brown by artist Linda Ridings. Braithwaite surrounded the table with hefty chairs adapted from one of her eighteenth-century English antique chairs. The beige linen slipcovers have noticeable texture and an even more noticeable $5/8$-inch welt. "I had never used a welt that thick," says the designer. "I wanted the chairs to have a very bold look."

In the living room, she set down two enormous sofas, each 42 inches deep, opposite one another. For their slipcovers she chose a creamy cotton matelassé: "It's a woven fabric with an antique look," she explains. A good old southern hunt board went on one side of the room;

on the other she placed a fine eighteenth-century Queen Anne chair. In this room pared of all ornament, the eye is drawn first to the antique woods, then to the rich, tactile surface of the slipcovers on the sofas.

From room to room, boldness is the primary quality that all the slipcovers convey. Severely tailored, rich in texture, the fabrics cloak the weighty furniture and give it a sculptural presence. Yet because of their unobtrusive colors, the slipcovers never overwhelm the eye, leaving the viewer to enjoy a house rich in fine antiques, well-proportioned rooms, and the very personal vision of its designer and owner.

"Simple and quiet" is the look Braithwaite wanted for the living room of her New England–style house. The proportions of the antique sawbuck table used as a coffee table called for upholstery of enormous scale (above).

The sofa slipcover, a cotton matelassé with a compass pattern, softens the pieces and helps blend their hefty size into the milk-colored room. In front of the hearth is an English chair outfitted in a white cotton slipcover

with diamond-shaped quilting. A wicker sofa (opposite) was sanded to an antique finish compatible with the mellow wood of the prized Queen Anne chair near it; it, too, is slipcovered in quilted white cotton.

The black linen slipcover on a wing chair lends a brooding, mysterious quality to the first-floor bedroom (opposite). "I wanted the house to look like America when the settlers first came," says designer Braithwaite.

The banquette in the family room (left) is slipcovered with a beige and white linen check that has the look and feel of an Early American homespun. For throw pillows, Braithwaite used bed pillows slipped into fine linen covers. She painted the room tavern-house brown to give it an intimate, cozy ambience.

TRANSFORMATIONS

O f all slipcovers' qualities, perhaps the most magical is their power to completely alter the appearance of furniture. If the upholstery of a sofa or chair is threadbare but the springs and filling still have bounce, a slipcover will instantly rescue the old seating and give it new life. If the lines of the old seating are not superb, a slipcover can transform them, too ~ adding a skirt to a boxy club chair with exposed wooden legs lends it a certain gracefulness and more pleasing proportions. Slipcovers can also mask the shape of a piece of furniture, turning one form into another that better suits the decorating agenda. With a simple cotton cover-up, a lightweight wicker chair can appear as substantial as a club chair, and a folding metal chair can pull rank at a party table. Of course, the most significant decorating transformation that slipcovers can work is the one designers have always valued: Like a new suit of clothes, fresh slipcovers on every piece can utterly change the look of an entire room. ❀

Second Seating: New Life for Old Furniture

Vintage chairs and sofas frequently offer marvelous shapes that slipcovers can show to advantage. The rakish curve of a Victorian slipper chair, the mushroom shape of a 1950s ottoman, the swelling roll arm of a 1940s love seat ~ duplicating such interesting shapes in new upholstery would probably mean spending thousands of dollars on a custom design. How much more clever and rewarding to discover a fabulously shaped piece at a consignment shop and vamp it up with a splendid slipcover. (Sturdiness of frame and inner construction should dictate the selection of a piece: A slipcover can camouflage many weaknesses, but it cannot make up for a wobbly foundation and sagging innards.) New seat cushions in shocking pink can reawaken a 1930s rattan sofa; a set of 1960s French provincial chairs will be reborn with black and white toile cover-ups tied to the seats.

To play up the very romantic shapes of a pair of love seats with continuous roll arms, Los Angeles designer Lynn von Kersting dressed them in loose slipcovers with gathered skirts that puddle on the floor. Before sewing it, she sun-bleached the rose-printed cotton so that it took on a faded look that suits the old-world style of the sofas.

Checked fabric has been popular since the eighteenth century. "I think every western European country has used it," says designer Richard C. Eustice. He appropriated the classic design in red and white for dining room seat covers with box-pleated skirts (above), then added a twentieth-century twist: Velcro fasteners.

Cherubs cavort on the pink and white slipcovers dressing up English mahogany dining chairs (opposite). For a touch of glamour, designers Ann Holden and Ann Dupuy covered the table with a silk cloth of raspberry and cream stripes.

On the wings of chairs:
A *covering of blue and
white striped cotton
allows an old wing chair
to blend in with the other
seating in a Swedish
country living room
(right). The simple
tailored slipcover,
designed with no skirt,
follows the sober form of
the upholstered chair.*

*A different approach
to wing chair dress-ups
was taken by a home-
owner in the living room
of his eighteenth-century
farmhouse (opposite).
The supple white cotton
cover on his fireside
chair gives the colonial
wing shape a decidedly
relaxed attitude.*

Once relegated to the back porch, a white wicker chaise was rejuvenated with a white cotton cover on the seat cushion and a down-filled back pillow ornamented with antique lace (right). The blue and white quilt adds a dash of pattern that echoes the basket-weave texture of the wicker furniture.

To create the look of a chaise in a bedroom, interior designer Ina Hoover slipcovered an easy chair in ruby red cotton (opposite). Then she turned an old ottoman into the chair's mate by using a cover-up of the ruby cotton secured with roping of the same fabric.

A loose slipcover with a
deeply flounced skirt
turns vintage upholstery
into a becoming little
boudoir chair in the New
York apartment of stylist
Tricia Foley (above).

Designer Vicente Wolf's
bench of gilded wood,
modeled after an antique
piece, goes casual with a
plain cotton canvas
cover secured with loose
string ties (opposite).

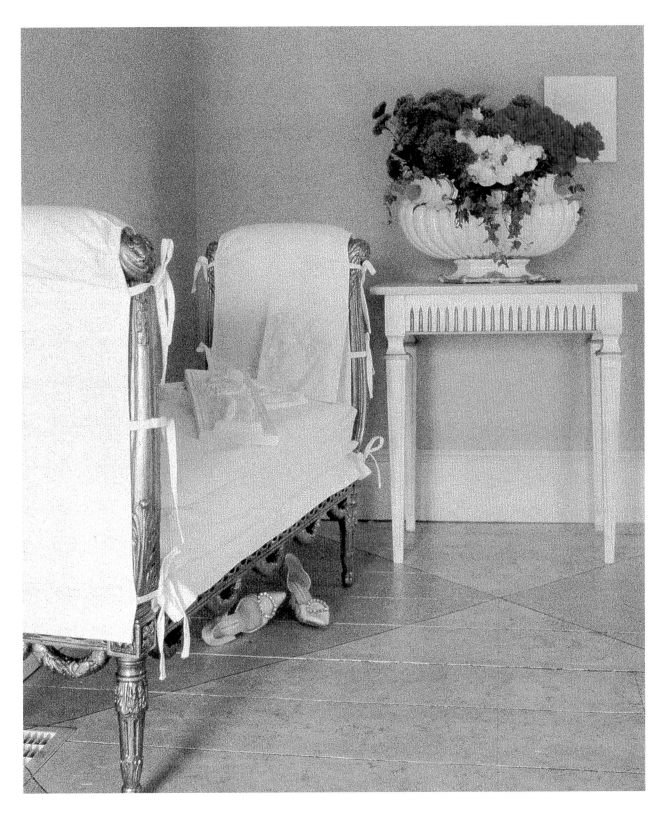

A chintz slipcover with full-blooming pink roses was designer William Diamond's idea for resuscitating an old white wicker chair (above). The cover for the boxed seat cushion has crisp white welting; the back cushion is finished with a coquettish ruffle. The informal wicker contrasts with the fine antique wing chair nearby, clad in George Washington toile.

Loosely constructed cotton slip-ons pulled over the headboard and footboard of an antique Swedish bed lend a cool look on warm summer days (opposite). A matching cover slipped over the chair seat completes the look. This technique can be used for seasonal changes, as here, or for a permanent transformation.

Manhattan designer Katherine Stephens gave a rustic willow chair city manners by adding a seat cushion slipcovered in a blue and white ribbon trellis pattern (left). Ties at each corner of the cushion hold it in place.

A woven rattan chair and love seat gained another season in the sun with seat and back cushions in vibrant aqua canvas (opposite). New zip-on covers of solid lavender and a print in pink, lavender, and green revived the worn throw pillows as well.

Clever Camouflages

Some of the most imaginative transformations are produced when slipcovers are tossed on objects other than seating. In the nineteenth century, it was fashionable to dress up mantels with pleated and draped material. Today, this idea could easily be adapted to bring texture and pattern to an undistinguished fireplace, and to avoid the expense of purchasing and installing a replacement mantel. Draped fabric is the easiest way to hide a sink's plumbing; an old bedroom dresser can be presssed into living room service just by slipping it into a piece of fabric; even walls can be "slipcovered" to disguise damaged plaster and exposed pipes that would be a major undertaking to correct structurally. Such creativity can take the place of otherwise costly makeovers and often requires little more than a sewing machine and some basic dressmaking techniques.

Following a style popular in the nineteenth century, a fall of fan-pleated cotton spills over a mantel in the historic Rotch-Jones-Duff House and Garden Museum in New Bedford, Massachusetts, dressing it up and giving it softer lines (opposite).

A checked sink skirt keeps the dishwasher under wraps in an eighteenth-century English kitchen (above). The camouflage was devised to prevent the sight of modern technology from intruding on the serenity of his retreat.

Designer Vicente Wolf devised a tailored cover-up for a battered old cabinet in blue and white striped cotton, adding a dark blue inverted pleat at the corners as a delineating detail (*above*).

Interior decorators David Easton and John Christensen revived an old chair with a beige cotton cover-up sporting a deep-pleated skirt (*opposite*). Then they "slipcovered" the walls as well, using a handsome beige and white striped cotton bought for $12 a yard. The fabric, which is hung from a hospital curtain track, drapes to the floor with a slight billow.

An overskirt of unlined linen, gathered at the top by a drawstring, hides an old lampshade and creates dappled light in the corner of designer David Parker's country living room (opposite).

Fabric tucked and draped like a ball gown gave the Cinderella treatment to a tiny washbasin in a powder room designed by decorative painters Natasha Bergreen and Liza Spierenburg (right). The draped fabric hides the sink's plumbing with a stylish flourish and underscores the fantasy effect of painted walls ornamented with a border of silver leaves.

Sitting Pretty in New Orleans

Like the homes of many designers, Ann Dupuy's is a proving ground for her ideas. When she first saw the huge three-bedroom apartment in the heart of uptown New Orleans, she was captivated by the airiness of the rooms and the light filtering through the trees outside. The second-story living room and dining area, with casement windows on three sides, were especially entrancing. Dupuy had the walls painted a luminous beige and pickled the floors a tone so pale that they are mostly shine. On this shimmering stage she arranged furniture displaying the classic lines she and her partner, Ann Holden, are known for: two eighteenth-century French bergères, a pair of contemporary armchairs, and an oval pearwood dining table from the 1940's. The designer also injected a chorus of offbeat notes that have become her signatures. She chose raffia upholstery for the traditional three-cushion down sofa in the living room, then plumped it up with silk throw pillows with antique fringe. On an adjacent wall she hung a gold-leafed antique cherub clutching a zany bent-wire sconce. But the *pièces de résistances* are her four wooden dining room chairs: Italian-made, they are dressed in formal slipcovers of pleated gold mesh reminiscent of ladies' tea gowns and looking very much like ingenues waiting for the next dance. The design, and the ironic debutante label, come from the drawing board of Dupuy and Holden.

Slipcovers have always been part of the Holden-Dupuy stock of decorating tricks. Working with a slipcover maker who aspired to be a couturier, the pair have designed chair covers of elegant silks and velvets adorned with belts, jewels, and rows of buttons up the back. "I like slipcovers because they make a chair something different from what it would ordinarily be," Dupuy explains. Indeed, the golden covers in the dining room totally transform the appearance of her straight-back chairs. They are the sort of tongue-in-cheek gesture that she relies on to keep her classic rooms from ever looking too self-important.

A lightweight linen cover-up relaxes a contemporary tub chair placed next to a raffia-upholstered sofa in designer Ann Dupuy's

New Orleans apartment. The beige linen blends well with the mood of the room, done in a lustrous palette of cream, beige, and gold tones.

"They looked like debutantes to me," says Dupuy of the pleated chemise dining chair covers she and her partner, Ann Holden, designed for Dupuy's apartment. Made of very finely woven metal mesh, they are translucent enough so that the crisscrossed backs of the wooden chairs underneath can be discerned.

Painted Fabric for an Artist's Studio

Georgia artist Ben Jennings produces decorative sisal carpets that are coveted by designers from New York to Los Angeles. The bright white studio in which he lives and works is a creative collage of found objects, recycled pieces, and his own paintings. Tucked behind a house in Buckhead, a tony section of northwest Atlanta, the flat-roofed building, with exterior grid walls like giant waffles, looks from the outside like a pop-art takeoff of a gas station; in fact, it was modeled after one. Jennings, who has a ready sense of humor, let wit be his guide in turning the 900-square-foot interior into a studio and home. Moving there after stints in New York and Boston, he reinvented what he had at hand, turning family hand-me-downs, friends' castoffs, and his college furniture into a unique assemblage for a true bachelor's paradise.

When the artist decided to rejuvenate a club chair and his "old college dinosaur" of a sofa, he created a slipcover fabric with his paintbrush. It started with 20 yards of Number 12-weight artist's canvas, softened with a good soak in an industrial washing machine. While the canvas was still wet, Jennings and an assistant unfurled half the yardage on a worktable, then stayed up most of the night painting huge swirls of black and white paint in frolicsome waves. "We wanted to keep it as playful as possible," says the artist. To make the brushwork stand out all the more, he slipcovered only the cushions of the chair and sofa in the swirling pattern; the body of the furniture is covered in white canvas as a contrast. Arranged around a Mies van der Rohe glass coffee table, the two pieces of upholstered furniture represent the essence of a living room, but one interpreted in the artist's wry, quirky manner.

Instead of serious accessories, Jennings has filled out his scheme with found objects that amuse the eye. Next to the sofa a pile of phone books is stacked like a cockeyed obelisk. And taking the place of honor usually reserved for an important bust on the coffee table, the artist has placed a fiberglass mannequin head wearing a jaunty lady's hat with a tulle veil.

"They feel like blue jeans," says artist Ben Jennings about the simple slipcovers he made from artist's canvas. The creative cover-ups give a matched look to an old beaten-up sofa and easy chair. The total investment: $600 for the fabric and sewing, plus a night of exuberant brushwork. The abstract painting over the bed is also by Jennings.

A tight, fitted construction keeps the furniture from having an obviously slip-covered look (opposite). Except for the painted pattern, the cover-ups are quite plain, with tailored kick pleats at the skirt back and corners. The jolt of color on the wall is a detail from a painting by Comer Jennings, the artist's father. The carved mirror and table at the entrance to the room (left) are family heirlooms. Jennings stenciled a seat cushion to revive the chair, discovered in his mother's attic.

FINE POINTS OF FABRIC

*f*abric gives the slipcover much of its character. A waffle-weave cotton in vibrant coral, a chintz of lush lilacs, a nubby linen with men's-shirt stripes ~ the distinctive look of each lends individuality to the slipcover and, in turn, to the room in which it is placed.

A few practical points are worth noting. For slipcovers that must withstand everyday use, a closely woven medium-weight fabric will hold up best. Natural fibers such as linen and cotton cling to upholstery much better than do synthetics. They also "breathe" and hold their shape well. In almost every setting, cotton is the best choice, as it is durable and easy to clean; fortunately, there is an enormous range of cottons to choose from. Linen, with its appealing texture, is another option, but since pure linen wrinkles easily, a better alternative for a slipcover that will get everyday use is a linen-cotton blend. Before any natural fabric is sewn up, it should be preshrunk; otherwise the slipcovers will be too snug after the first laundering. ✾

The Beauty of Chintz

Chintz, a classic slipcover favorite, is a cotton, either printed or solid, that is finished with a shiny glazed suface. It drapes with the relaxed and stylish insouciance that slipcovers should convey, it is hard-wearing, and it is easily cleaned. The tightly woven cotton fiber shows off the radiance of color printing in a way few other textiles do.

In the 1700s, when chintz was brought to Europe from the East Indies, it became the rage in decorating fashion. Eventually, as English and French textile manufacturers developed their own versions, it evolved into a classic fabric for the European interior. During the 1800s, European chintz was imported to America, where it was often used for slipcovers. By the turn of the century the fashion for chintz was at an all-time high, and by the 1920s, American decorator Elsie de Wolfe had popularized offbeat designs and colors ~ red and green parrots on a black ground, pink roses on a mauve ground ~ as well as the traditional soft-toned florals.

In more recent times, it was English decorator John Fowler who really brought chintz into the sunlight. He loved the printed cotton for its "humble elegance" and was especially fond of the delicate colors of English chintz. A loose-fitting chintz slipcover, printed with watercolor-tinted flowers, was always at home in a Fowler room.

Today there are chintz prints for every taste and decor, many of which are based on nineteenth-century French and English designs. The most beautifully printed examples may display scores of colors in a single length of fabric. The patterns of floral chintzes can range from full-blown exotic lilies to sedate, diminutive primroses. There are romantic floral chintzes on delicate, powder-colored grounds and vibrant perennials blooming on deep-toned backgrounds of green, brown, and ~ most dramatic of all ~ black. Nonfloral chintzes can be amusing, strewn with oriental vases, spotted giraffes, musical instruments, or King Charles spaniels.

Embellished with ruffles and trims, a chintz slipcover can look as ornate as an eighteenth-century ball gown. Yet even the most tailored cover-up will have élan when cut from an exquisitely printed chintz.

London designer Charles Beresford-Clark designed a thoroughly English tailored sack to cover the sofa in the living room of his country house.

The cream ground of the rosy chintz is the light stroke the room needs to make it click; a dark slipcover would have dulled the scheme.

Two printed chintzes, both awash in perennial blooms, were chosen by interior decorator Nicholas Haslam for the garden room in a famous English country retreat once owned by legendary designer John Fowler. Although the print on the sofa slipcovers is different from the one on the armchair cushions, the two strike a harmony because they share white backgrounds and similar red and green colors.

In a Los Angeles cabana, designer Lynn von Kersting rejuvenated an old chaise with a cover blossoming with blush roses on an inky background. The dark hue of the chintz relates beautifully to the black chest and coffee table and the ebony-toned frames on the wall.

Huge bouquets of tulips and roses that could have been stolen from a Dutch floral painting enliven the furniture in this weekend house (above and opposite). By slipcovering the large sofa and tiny slipper chair in the same fabric, both with full gathered skirts edged in blue and white stripes, the owner gave an en suite appearance to two pieces of quite dissimilar scale and proportion and brought harmony to the room.

On Solid Ground

Several white fabrics collaborate in a summery Manhattan boudoir created by designer Noel Jeffrey He used scalloped slipcovers of creamy cotton damask to dress an elegant antique bench and gilded armchair. Then he tossed two tableskirts, one of textured cotton matelassé, the other of gossamer-fine linen, on a plain round table to create a sumptuous nightstand.

In a room with a profusion of patterns, upholstery slipcovered in a solid-colored fabric will have a restful effect. In a setting with one or several floral fabrics on furnishings and windows, one or two chairs slipcovered in a solid color pulled from the print can lend richness.

A neutral-colored fabric will work with most schemes, and pale neutrals in particular are wonderful for summer slipcovers: A room filled with furniture sheathed in all-white or all-beige cover-ups is the visual equivalent of an icy glass of lemonade. In general, a neutral colored fabric is even more interesting if it has texture ~ quilted cotton, cotton damask, and linen, for example, all provide tactile interest and surface dimension.

When working with strong-colored fabrics, texture is less of a consideration than it is with neutrals ~ a red cotton looks rich on its own, even when the fabric is a duck or sailcloth that lacks surface texture. With all solid fabrics, quality of workmanship is especially important. Crooked seams or a slightly off-kilter skirt can be camouflaged by the bunches of flowers on a printed fabric, but on a solid-colored one, whether neutral or bright, sewing that is off the mark can leave the slipcover looking that way, too.

Nantucket designer George Davis brought together a number of subtle textures in a living room of pale brown and beige (opposite). The armchair of split rattan is a study in texture in its own right: Cushions are slipcovered in linen herringbone borrowed from a haberdashery; a welt of camel suede adds polish. The sofa, wearing an oatmeal-colored cotton and linen blend, is finished with the same suede piping.

Using a single solid-colored fabric to cover all the seating in a room always achieves a calming and harmonious look. Hyacinth blue as fresh as a spring crocus was designer Nancy Braithwaite's choice for all the furniture in a living room filled with rattan furniture (above).

Mixed Prints

Slipcovering chairs and sofas in a mélange of prints, stripes, and checks creates a pleasing, carefree look. The mixture of patterns signals a nonchalant attitude, and people always seem to gravitate to rooms dressed this way. Playing prints against one another is a technique that lies at the heart of the English country style. American interior designers have coaxed the process along by using more brightly colored patterns rather than the subdued ones that the English seem to prefer and by including bold geometrics to energize the scene.

The most unexpected combinations of prints and geometrics will blend if they share similar hues and tonal values. Arranging the room so that there is a balance of color and scale among the slipcovered pieces, curtains, and other fabric patterns assures harmony. In these rooms, pillows slipcovered in the odd stripe or print act as exclamation points, adding wit to the fabric mix.

A French metal garden chair turns into whimsical seating at a breakfast table (opposite), thanks to a blue and white striped cotton popover and a fringed cushion made from a 1940s tablecloth in a contrasting print.

By mixing vintage cotton and chintz fabrics in large- and small-scale prints dominated by red tones, designer Lynn von Kersting created a cheerful breakfast spot (left).

The checked cotton chambray slipcover of a little wing chair is part of a lively orchestration of checks and stripes by designer Barbara Ostrom in this American country living room (above). Holding all the patterns together are the reds and blues that dominate on most of the fabrics. The deft placement of the patterns also results in a harmonious effect, helping to anchor the scheme and keep it from teetering off balance.

A sweet coral and white wallpaper might seem too dainty a choice to team with bench cushions in a print of acid-green leaves and berries (opposite). But the mix works, thanks to the addition of smaller checked and striped pillows that are edged with the berries-and-leaves fabric. Also notable are the overscale checks of the tablecloth, which balance the large grid of the wallpaper.

Extravagance by the Yard

On furniture intended to be admired but sel-dom, if ever, sat upon ~ fragile but life-size works of art, in the words of one designer ~ slip-covers of luxurious linen velvet, silk damask, or brocade velvet are all that will do. For a shapely chair frame that is meant to be glimpsed, a diaphanous fabric is certainly a fitting indul-gence; organdy, chiffon, a delicately pleated synthetic, or a piece of gold-thread sari silk are all worthy choices. On a straight-back chair, a gossamer slipcover, in fabric as delicate as a drag-onfly's wing, will introduce mystery and a flutter of fantasy to any interior.

Unusual fabrics ~ an elaborately quilted white cotton or a cut velvet, for example ~ are not ideal for everyday use as they don't stand up to wear and must be dry-cleaned rather than laundered. However, for the extra measure of attention they require, they can provide an exceptional touch in any room.

The seductive shape of a Louis XV–style side chair peeks out through a gauzy silk slipcover (opposite). On this simply cut slip-cover, the shadow stripes in the silk fabric lend ornamental richness.

For a room that sparkles with mirrors, gilded ornaments, and twinkling lights, New Orleans designer Mario Villa chose metal arm-chairs and a shell-shaped chaise (above). The vanilla damask covers on the cushions are subtly luxurious, perfect for seating that is as finely wrought as platinum jewelry.

A pair of French provincial upholstered side chairs took on decorative importance when they were done up in slipcovers emblazoned with baskets spilling over with fruit. Although the fabric looks hand-stenciled, it is actually a printed cotton. Centering the fruit motif on the chair back, then repeating it on the seat, gives the treatment a dramatic effect. The skirt was fashioned from the running border of the fabric. An equally unusual look could be achieved by stenciling a central motif on plain cream-colored cotton covers or by snipping out a design from a printed fabric and appliquéing it to a plain cover-up.

Dressed in gray-green quilted cotton seat covers with a satiny finish, the black lacquer chairs in designer Thomas Beeton's Los Angeles dining room are ready for a tea party. In this space, rich in elegant ornamental detail ~ a stylized wave border, voluptuous painted urns, a heavily fringed damask tablecloth ~ quilted fabric brings an appropriate touch of splendor to the chairs. As a shimmering detail, Beeton stitched dangling antique chandelier crystals at the corners of the slightly gathered chair skirts.

Three Looks for a Weekend House

Guests who come to the country house of John Brewer and Ken LaCroix for a party on Memorial Day often don't recognize the living room when they return for dinner after Labor Day. What they assume to be a complete redecoration is really a new scheme worked with the zip of a slipcover. Three sets of slipcovers, to be precise.

The flexibility that slipcovers can offer in decorating is a theme well known to Brewer and LaCroix, owners of a decorator-fabric firm in New York. Their Connecticut weekend house started life as a barn in the 1880s and was converted to a house in the 1940s. "It was in terrible condition," Brewer recalls, with a 40-year-old kitchen, a 40-year-old bathroom, and wiring and plumbing to match.

Brewer and LaCroix completely renovated the house. The living room, featuring 17-foot ceilings and a stone mantel with a yawning five-foot hearth, received new French doors and a lunette window above them. To stand up to the cavernous space, the homeowners designed furniture of enormous proportions. At four feet by six feet, the coffee table is the size of an apartment foyer. The roll-arm sofa is eight feet long, and the rest of

To keep the enclosed porch from looking predictable, John Brewer and Ken LaCroix chose rattan seating in a variety of shapes, then had slipcovers made in a mix of cotton fabrics. The slip-ons can be easily whisked off for cleaning or a change of mood.

the seating is equally gargantuan. "When I first saw the furniture I thought I'd made a mistake," says Brewer. Once in place, though, the seating looked just right; anything smaller would have been dwarfed by the huge room.

Because the seating was tailor-made for the space, it is an investment the owners will not soon replace. But they *can* change the slipcovers. In summer, the whole living room goes light when beige and white covers are slipped on. A second set, in gray and white, provides another neutral look. Fall and winter warm to a third set of dress-ups and pillow shams made from ten different French cottons with dramatic large prints and geometric patterns in a spicy mix of red and mustard yellow. The colors and motifs of the fabrics, based on eighteenth-century country French designs, suit the sophisticated rusticity of the renovated barn.

So pleased were the owners with the living room's slipcovered decor that they extended the look throughout the house. For the rattan porch furniture, they made seat cushion cover-ups from cotton printed with a cornucopia of ripe fruit on a paisley ground. And when guests relax on the teak chaises by the pool, the standard-issue white canvas cushions that came with the recliners are concealed by exotic-colored slipcovers of French cotton. Set amid the hot pink roses on a June day, the chairs give the yard the totally unexpected look of a lush Caribbean garden.

The strong play of pattern in the slipcovers stands up to the vastness of Brewer and LaCroix's living room (left). All the covers have the tailored, tidy fit of permanent upholstery, along with pencil-width welting that traces every edge and curve. The eight-foot sofa wears a mustard-colored cotton with a charcoal gray and cream-colored pattern complemented by a cream-colored welt. The slipper chair in the foreground is covered in a cotton in an ikat pattern, a wavy design often seen on flat-weave rugs.

"Envelopes" sewn from exotic-looking printed cotton fit snugly over plain cushions and transform two mail-order chaises into striking poolside seating (above).

DECORATIVE DETAILS

he similarities between slipcover styles and the art of dressmaking become even more apparent when it comes to decorative details. A slipcover skirt can assume all the shapes invented by the seamstress, cascading into a series of narrow knife pleats or falling in a row of broad box pleats; it can be gathered all the way around like a demure dirndl or caught at intervals like the lush billows of a dance gown. Imaginatively applied trims produce stylish effects in slipcovers, just as they do in haute couture ~ decorative ribbon to finish a hem, yards of grosgrain sewn as a ribbony trellis covering the entire surface. Rosettes, tassels, and swags draw attention to the outlines of the furniture or the voluptuous colors of the fabric. Bows, buttons, and string ties turn the practical work of fastening a slipcover into an opportunity for artful embellishment. And, like icing on a cake, pillows treated in an exceptional manner ~ hand-painted fabric, embroidery, or silk-fringed damask, for example ~ are always a striking, and welcoming, accessory for the exquisitely trimmed slipcover. ❁

A Touch of
Haute Couture

Elegant silk braids, rosettes, fabric bows, and baubles, which dressmakers have used since before the eighteenth century, are also part of the classic vocabulary of upholstery and slipcover embellishment. The French have a delightful name for the sum total of woven and braided trims: passementerie. Included in this category is gimp, a flat braid used as border edging that can be quite simple or very elaborate; cord, which may be delicate piping or thick rope to swag around a skirt; and rosettes and tassels, which can serve as punctuation points. Some of the most beautiful passementerie is handmade in France and England. Once sold exclusively through decorator trade sources, fine upholstery trims are now readily available in home furnishings and retail fabric shops. Applied with a discerning eye, these silky trims enrich the surface of a slipcover and give it immeasurable flair.

Buttons and bows in particular are borrowed from the dressmaker's dummy. A row of buttons up the back of a chair or plump bows at the corners of a sofa skirt are charming touches; the same ones used in dressmaking can be stitched to a slipcover. Fabric-covered buttons, easily made with supplies from a notions shop, provide a polished accent. Grosgrain, velvet, and other decorative ribbons can be used to make bows.

Even better, because it stands up well to wear, is a bow constructed of the same print or solid as the slipcover, or a boldly contrasting fabric.

The skirt is perhaps the most frequently used slipcover detailing. Tightly gathered so that it billows out like a taffeta dance dress, sewn in saucy pleats like the edges of a flapper's chemise, cut with scalloped edges ~ whatever the style, the length of the skirt should be dictated by the proportions of the chair or sofa for which it is destined. A chair of some heft or with a tall back usually calls for a skirt with some length so that it looks balanced. However, a skirt length can be exaggerated for whimsical results ~ a cover-up sewn with a slightly long gathered skirt can be charming on a little slipper chair. For gathered, pleated, and ruffled skirts, a lighter-weight fabric is the best choice because it drapes well and is pliable; heavier-weight fabrics don't take to pleating and gathering very well, but are fine for a novelty treatment like a scalloped-edged skirt meant to hang straight. Practicality should also be a consideration in selecting skirt styles. For a chair that gets daily use, a floor-sweeping ruffle can be impractical, getting in the way of children's feet, the family dog, and the general traffic of life.

Boston designer Ingrid Goulston transformed her own home into a charming Scandinavian-style setting. In a room with a traditional Swedish sofa bed, white wooden chairs are softened with tie-on cushions covered in checked cotton. Deep ruffles around the edges flounce over the seats.

Elaborately constructed slipcovers display a grandeur that matches the baroque forms of the armchair and camelback settee they dress. The high-back chair wears a cover in a damask-printed linen ending in scalloped "tongues" over a beige and white striped linen skirt. Two closures assure its form-hugging fit: a concealed zipper up the chair back and, for the skirt flap, a fabric fastener under one chair arm. Softening the formality of the stately seventeenth-century–style settee is a chalk-white slipcover of cotton and linen.

Cream-colored cotton slipcovers falling in a burst of saucy pleats enliven a dining area furnished with mahogany seating. The kicky pleats, trimmed in mulberry cotton, bring a sense of movement to the staid Empire-style chairs.

In a classic Rhode Island shingle house designed by architect Oliver Cope, strikingly deep skirts were stitched to sofa and easy chair slipcovers in an over-scale cotton print. Also distinctive is the sky-blue banding at the tops and hems of the gathered skirts. Fabric for the back cushions of the sofas was cut and sewn so that the print matches from cushion to cushion.

Designer Sandy Ceppos turned a slightly worn wing chair into a pretty little boudoir seat by dressing it in a floral slipcover with a deep skirt gathered like a frilly dirndl (opposite).

A simple oyster-white linen slipcover dresses a mahogany chair copied from a Russian antique (opposite); an inch-wide binding in a red and white Greek key motif provides a striking edging. One of antiquity's most popular designs, the Greek key is also a subtle reference to another neo-classical element in this setting ~ the lyre base on the mappa burl desk, a reproduction of one in Czar Nicholas I's library.

The Biedermeier arm-chairs that architect Peter Pennoyer brought to his marriage to designer Katie Ridder sported red leather seats that didn't suit the couple's new apartment (above). Ridder devised a clever camouflage using simple white duck cover-ups fastened with Velcro and edged with black grosgrain ribbon she purchased for a dollar a yard in Manhattan's millinery district. The grosgrain accentuates the ebonized wood on the chairs; the white slipcovers, says Ridder, give the antique seating "the softness I wanted."

Taking his stitches from a Chanel suit once owned by the Duchess of Windsor, designer Scott Salvator ran a row of coquettish bows up the back of a pink linen slipcover for a dressing table chair. Edged with an inch-wide border of white fabric neatly mitered at the corners, the slipcover falls in a kick pleat, like a woman's skirt.

Caught with decorative bows at each side, red and white striped slip-covers of quilted cotton transform spare chairs for a dinner party at fashion designer Carolina Herrera's Manhattan apartment. The chairs are set up in a dressing room tented in toile de Jouy.

All-white chair covers
with seamstress's details,
including a self-welt and
fabric-covered buttons,
have the understated
chic of a strand of good
pearls worn with a
simple sweater. Dallas
designer Charlotte Comer
used the plump welt as a
way to define the curvy
shapes of breakfast
room chairs in a 1930s
Spanish colonial.
Her choice of natural
white cotton fabric is
a sound match for
the room's robust and
unfussy architecture.

Designer Vicente Wolf added a big pouch pocket to a white cotton canvas cover-up to keep magazines within handy reach. Long ties threaded through grommets on the pocket and stitched to the back as fasteners give the chair a whimsical quality. The back cushion cover is gathered in a few soft pleats at the corners. That finish, called a Turkish corner, is usually used on a cushion of silk or velvet; on ordinary canvas slip-covers it is an unexpected stroke of luxury.

Pillow Art

As an ornament, a pillow introduces color, texture and dimension to the seating it adorns. A pillow is also a welcome backrest; sinking into its softness makes any chair more inviting, all the more so if the pillow is filled with down, feathers, or a combination of the two.

Mapping out designs for decorative pillows beforehand is helpful in planning the total look of a slipcovered sofa or chair. One possible tactic is underplaying the slipcover in favor of very ornamental or colorful pillows: A plain white cotton duck slipcover is the ideal background for a bevy of pillows in hot Caribbean colors; a cream damask is enriched by a profusion of damask and velvet squares, rounds, and rectangles in jewel tones trimmed with gilt braid, fringe, and soutache embroidery. Another ploy is to use quite simple pillows to play second fiddle to a slipcover cut from an overscale, vividly colored print. In this scheme, a few pillows in solid colors might pick up on and underline the predominant tones in the print.

Some pillows are works of art in their own right. Designer Mary Douglas Drysdale's handmade pillows are virtuoso displays of craftsmanship, color, and shape. She concentrated more on the architectural aspects of interiors than on the dressmaker arts, but then reached a point in her work at which she wanted to use extraordinary pillows to energize her rooms, in much the way she employed contemporary paintings and exceptional antique furniture. The pillows introduce "pattern and color and they really animate rooms in an exciting way," she says. For motifs she turned to books on architectural ornament and pattern design. "You can abstract pieces of a pattern and put them together your own way," she explains. An admirer of the arts of stencil and appliqué, she likes to "take old construction techniques and reinvent them." Lately she has been designing pillows in fine silks with elaborate appliqués and decorative borders. Constructed like slipcovers, they slide over feather and down pillows with the ease of a silk blouse. For closures, the covers have buttons that slip into exquisite handmade buttonholes. "The man who makes them comes from a long line of Viennese tailors," explains Drysdale.

For sofa pillows, designer Mary Douglas Drysdale cut motifs from solid-colored cotton chintz and appliquéd them to chintz backgrounds. She chose finely stitched polka-dot cushions for two antique chairs. Designs on the long skinny pillow are based on heraldic devices.

Making a graphic state-
ment: In a June-fresh
blue and white room,
designer William Diamond
chose crisp white welting
on vibrant royal-blue
cushions (above). He
tossed in two huge blue
and white checked
pillows to sharpen the
decorative message.

In a sunny breakfast
room, designer Nancy
Braithwaite used plain
white cotton on the wicker
chair seats, then ran a
double line of bright red
piping around the edges
(opposite). For the back
pillows she chose red and
white striped cotton as
bold as a barber pole.

On a champagne-colored damask sofa slipcover (left), designer Elizabeth Speert carried the idea of understated luxury one step further by adding throw pillows of copper, bronze, and matte-gold silk damask trimmed with thick fringe in the same faded metallic tones.

In another treatment of a cream-colored sofa, a profusion of pillows is all the more interesting because of the diversity of black and white fabrics, including toile, plaid, and a print of trees (below left).

In a bathroom designed by decorator Mariette Himes Gomez (opposite), an antique metal garden chair is warmed by a square floral-printed pillow in muted colors on a cinnamon ground. The thick welt around the edges gives it substance enough to stand alone.

In her Paris duplex, textile designer Dominique Kieffer completed a richly layered look with piles of pillows on luxuriously overscale sofas. A pair of brilliantly striped cushions enlivens one sofa of dark cotton jacquard; reinforcements are stacked up on a bookshelf behind. A pale roll-arm sofa is plumped up with half a dozen pillows in jacquard and checked fabrics in soothing beige tones.

On a slipcovered old sofa, designer Mariette Himes Gomez used a variety of pillow shapes and sizes to introduce color and pattern to the palomino-toned landscape of her Manhattan living room (right).

Salvaged from a damaged Aubusson carpet, an oblong cushion is a delightful sliver of ruby-toned pattern, in rich contrast to the very simple white settee (below). When a cushion's textile is elaborate, a simple edging like this red cord is all the detail that is needed.

DIRECTORY OF DESIGNERS AND ARCHITECTS

Thomas Beeton
Thomas M. Beeton, Inc.
Beverly Hills, California

Charles Beresford-Clark
Charles Beresford-Clark, Inc.
London, England

Natasha Bergreen
New York, New York

Laura Bohn
Lembo Bohn Design Associates
New York, New York

Nancy Braithwaite
Nancy Braithwaite Interiors, Inc.
Atlanta, Georgia

Dan Carithers
Atlanta, Georgia

Sandy Ceppos
Designs for the Home
New Canaan, Connecticut

Steven Charlton
Goodman Charlton
Los Angeles, California

John Christensen
David Anthony Easton, Inc.
New York, New York

Charlotte Comer
Charlotte Comer Interiors
  and Collectibles
Dallas, Texas

Oliver Cope
Oliver Cope Architects
New York, New York

George Davis
Weeds
Nantucket, Massachusetts

William Diamond
William Diamond Design
New York, New York

Mary Douglas Drysdale
Drysdale Design Associates, Inc.
Washington, D.C.

Anne Dupuy
Holden & Dupuy
New Orleans, Louisiana

David Easton
David Anthony Easton, Inc.
New York, New York

Beverly Ellsley
Beverly Ellsley Interiors
Westport, Connecticut

Mary Emmerling
Mary Emmerling, Inc.
New York, New York

Richard C. Eustice
Boston, Massachusetts

Heather Faulding
Faulding Associates
New York, New York

Beverly Field
Beverly Field Interiors
Dallas, Texas

Tricia Foley
Tricia Foley Designs
New York, New York

Isabel Fowlkes
New York, New York

Mariette Himes Gomez
Gomez Associates
New York, New York

Jeffrey Goodman
Goodman Charlton
Los Angeles, California

Ingrid Goulston
Ingrid Interiors
Boston, Massachusetts

Carol Gramm
Gramm Design
Garrison, New York

Nicholas Haslam
Nicholas Haslam, Inc.
London, England

Ann Holden
Holden & Dupuy
New Orleans, Louisiana

Ina Hoover
Charleston, South Carolina

Noel Jeffrey
Noel Jeffrey, Inc.
New York, New York

Joseph Lembo
Lembo Bohn Design Associates
New York, New York

Gary Lovejoy
Gary Lovejoy Associates
Washington, D.C.

Ronald Mayne
Steingray Hornsby Antiques
  and Interiors
Watertown, Connecticut

Chris O'Connell
Chris O'Connell, Inc.
Santa Fe, New Mexico

Barbara Ostrom
Barbara Ostrom Associates, Inc.
Mahwah, New Jersey

David Parker
Pound Ridge, New York

Peter Pennoyer
Peter Pennoyer Architects
New York, New York

Katie Ridder
Katie Ridder, Inc.
New York, New York

John Saladino
John F. Saladino, Inc.
New York, New York

Scott Salvator
Scott Salvator, Inc.
New York, New York

De Bare Saunders
Steingray Hornsby Antiques
  and Interiors
Watertown, Connecticut

Michael Smith
Michael Smith, Inc.
Beverly Hills, California

Charles Spada
Charles Spada Interiors
Boston, Massachusetts

Elizabeth Speert
Elizabeth Speert, Inc.
Boston, Massachusetts

Liza Spierenburg
New York, New York

Katherine Stephens
Katherine Stephens Associates, Inc.
New York, New York

Tom Vanderbeck
Hadlyme, Connecticut

Mario Villa
Mario Villa Gallery
New Orleans, Louisiana

Lynn von Kersting
Indigo Seas
Los Angeles, California

Vicente Wolf
Vicente Wolf Associates
New York, New York

The room on page 2 was designed by Ann Dupuy and Ann Holden; page 4, Isabel Fowlkes; page 7, designed by Heather Faulding and decorated by Carol Gramm; page 11, Nancy Braithwaite; page 13, Dominique Kieffer; page 14, Michael Smith; page 32, John Saladino; page 48, Nancy Braithwaite; page 64, Ann Dupuy and Ann Holden; page 118, Charles Beresford-Clark; page 142, Mariette Himes Gomez.

PHOTOGRAPHY CREDITS

1	James Cooper	56	Dominique Vorillon	104	Lilo Raymond
2	Lizzie Himmel	57	Judith Watts	105	Jeff McNamara
4	Edgar de Evia	58	Jack Winston	106	John Vaughan
7	Kari Haavisto	60-63	Jack Winston	107	Jack Winston
8	Antoine Bootz	64	Langdon Clay	108	Kari Haavisto
11	Jeff McNamara	66-67	Jack Winston	109	Tom McCavera
13	Thibault Jeanson	68	Edgar de Evia	110	James Cooper
14	Jeremy Samuelson	69	Langdon Clay	111	Andrew Boyd
16	Lizzie Himmel	70	Thibault Jeanson	112	Tom McCavera
18	Jeff McNamara	71	Joe Standart	113	Tim Street-Porter
19	Langdon Clay	72	Kari Haavisto	114	Elizabeth Zeschin
20	Tria Giovan	73	Michael Dunne	116-117	Elizabeth Zeschin
21	Jack Winston	74	Antoine Bootz	118	Michael Dunne
22	Kari Haavisto	75	James Cooper	120	Michael Skott
22-23	Jeff McNamara	76	Lizzie Himmel	122	James Cooper
24-25	Fran Brennan	77	Elyse Lewin	123	Antoine Bootz
26	Jeremy Samuelson	78	Jeff McNamara	124	Judith Watts
28-31	Jeremy Samuelson	79	David Frazier	125	Lizzie Himmel
32	Kari Haavisto	80	Kari Haavisto	126	Kari Haavisto
34	Antoine Bootz	81	Michael Dunne	127-128	Antoine Bootz
36-37	James Merrell	82	Jeff McNamara	129	Thibault Jeanson
38	Jon Jensen	83	Antoine Bootz	130	Fran Brennan
39	Jeff McNamara	84	Nancy Hill	131	Jeff McNamara
40	Kit Latham	85	Antoine Bootz	132	Judith Watts
41	David Frazier (top)	86	Langdon Clay	134	Lizzie Himmel
	Kit Latham (bottom)	88-89	Langdon Clay	135	Langdon Clay
42	Gordon Beall	90	Walter Smalling	136	Peter Margonelli (top)
43	Gordon Beall	92-93	Walter Smalling		Tom McWilliam
44-47	Kari Haavisto	94	Elizabeth Zeschin		(bottom)
48	Jack Winston	96	Michael Dunne	137	Jeff McNamara
50-51	Karen Radkai	98	Michael Dunne	138	Thibault Jeanson
52	Jeff McNamara	99	Jack Winston	139	Thibault Jeanson
53	Kari Haavisto	100-101	William P. Steele		(top and bottom)
54-55	Chris Mead	102-103	Jeff McNamara		

INDEX

ACKNOWLEDGMENTS

House Beautiful would like to thank the following homeowners: Deborah and Joseph DiCintio (pages 1, 75, 110, 122), Chase and Katherine Sanderson (pages 26-31), Barbara Deichman (pages 36-37), Marilyn Caldwell (page 40), Angela Maccapani (pages 50-51), Ellen O'Neill (page 52), Renny Reynolds (page 70), William Thuillier (page 81), Ben Jennings (pages 90-93), J. Hyde Crawford (page 100), John Brewer and Ken LaCroix (pages 94, 114-117), Carolina Herrera (page 129), Dominique Kieffer (page 138).

The photographs on pages 32, 44, and 47 were taken at the Kips Bay Boys' Club Decorator Show House; page 41, the Kips Bay Boys' and Girls' Club Decorator Show House; page 68, the Junior League of Boston Decorators' Show House; page 73, the Charlestown Show House; page 83, the Royal Oak Foundation; page 85, the Royal Oak Foundation; page 102, the Rogers Memorial Library Designer Showcase; page 111, the Junior League of New Orleans Decorators' Show House; page 128, the Royal Oak Foundation; page 138, the Historic Preservation for Tarrant County, Texas Design Showcase (Fort Worth).